SO-DZP-930

Writing to Learn
Across the Curriculum

by
John W. Myers

Library of Congress Catalog Card Number 84-61203
ISBN 0-87367-209-7
Copyright ©1984 by the Phi Delta Kappa Educational Foundation
Bloomington, Indiana

This fastback is sponsored by the Tennessee Technological University Chapter of Phi Delta Kappa, which made a generous contribution toward publication costs.

The chapter sponsors this fastback as a special tribute to deceased members of the chapter and in honor of all members of the chapter.

Table of Contents

A Definition

Writing to learn is not learning to write. The English teacher is concerned with the "nuts and bolts" of written composition: grammar, spelling, sentence structure, and all the rest. But the emphasis of writing to learn is on learning content, not the writing skills themselves, although writing skills are likely to improve through practice. In this approach writing is a vehicle for clear and logical communication. It is a process in which thinking — the organization, evaluation, and synthesis of knowledge — is essential. The teacher using this approach need not spend time looking for spelling errors and comma faults, but is concerned with the quality of ideas expressed and the clarity with which they are expressed.

Writing to learn is based on a growing body of research into the writing process that suggests that writing can be a powerful strategy for learning content. The student who participates in a writing to learn program is likely to learn more content, understand it better, and retain it longer. As a bonus, writing skills are also likely to improve through use.

Ideally, writing to learn in the content areas is complemented by an effective learning to write program in the English classroom. The result of the two is synergistic — the sum of the two parts working together is greater than either working alone. Writing to learn and learning to write are two sides of the same coin in the secondary school. They are both important.

A Rationale

Some years ago, the public became concerned about the reading skills of children; the news media proclaimed that "Johnny can't read." Well, we are still concerned about Johnny and Jane as readers, but we have also become concerned about their other communication skills. We have found that Johnny and Jane are not particularly effective as writers.

In the case of reading, a good deal of research has appeared concerning the nature of the reading process. One of the results of that research has been a new emphasis on teaching reading in the content areas at the secondary school level. Today we are following the same path in relation to writing skills.

We are just beginning to learn about the writing process. For many teachers, writing is simply a transcribing process that generates a product on paper. This product is then graded by the teacher of English, marked with a red pen, and returned to the student for possible correction or revision. This approach to teaching writing has not proven to be effective. Through the pioneering work of James Britton, Janet Emig, and others, we are learning to view writing as a complex mental process — a process that can be used by teachers as a powerful tool to enhance learning in all subject areas.

Writing should be an integral part of any instructional program. It is unfortunate that, outside the English classroom, most teachers provide only limited writing opportunities for their students, usually in the form of note-taking or an occasional essay question on an exam. Writing can do much more. Properly used, it can become the single most powerful tool a teacher can employ.

The writing to learn approach is sufficiently established to warrant investigation by all secondary school teachers. This fastback is intended to help teachers understand and implement the writing to learn approach. The approach does not steal time from instruction; it enhances and clarifies instructional content. It encourages student thought and the synthesis of knowledge in the content areas. The approach does not ask other teachers to do the job of the English teacher; it is not intended to teach only writing skills. However, the approach can pay big dividends in the quality of learning. The result of the approach is improved learning, not just improved writing.

Writing to Learn in the Content Areas

Although the English teacher may choose to integrate learning to write and writing to learn, teachers in other content areas using the writing to learn approach should not dwell on grammar, spelling, or other technical aspects of language. The general rule should be: *If it does not interfere with clarity of meaning, ignore it.* The demands of learning content require that technical matters be de-emphasized except where they interfere with the clear transmission of ideas. This is not to say that a teacher could not reasonably expect students to spell correctly those terms that are unique to a given content area, e.g., in biology such terms as "mitosis" and "osmosis." Each teacher must decide when a given technical error is worth bringing to the student writer's attention. But under no circumstances should the teacher read through a student's paper deliberately looking for each misspelling, comma fault, or missing period. In evaluating writing, there is a tendency to slip into this habit, rather than to evaluate the quality of the content.

The teacher using the writing to learn approach needs to be concerned with ideas and their clear presentation. Evaluation should be based on the completeness, logic, and clarity of the thoughts expressed. Teachers need to determine whether the student writer understands what he is writing about; whether the information cited is correct, complete, and logically presented; and whether the work reflects real thought on the part of the student. If teachers conduct this type of evaluation of student writing, there is simply not time to deal with the mechanics of writing.

In a well-articulated program there should be cooperation between the faculty involved in teaching the mechanics of writing and those using the writing to learn approach in the content areas. For example, a science teacher concerned about a grammatical problem in a student's lab report might refer the problem to the appropriate English teacher. This puts the English teacher in the unique position of helping students both to learn to write and to write to learn; the problems inherent in balancing those two roles will be addressed elsewhere in this fastback.

Student writers should also be aware that they write for a variety of audiences: teachers, themselves, other students, and assorted other individuals. When using the writing to learn approach, it is the responsibility of the content area teacher to ensure that students know for whom they are writing. It is the English teacher's role to ensure that, once the audience is known, the student has some idea of how to proceed.

What can teachers do in their classrooms to capitalize on the writing to learn approach? There are dozens of ways to integrate writing activities into content areas at the secondary level. The following list by Stephen Tchudi has a method applicable for every content area:

Content Area Writing Activities*

Journals and diaries (real or imaginary)
Biographical sketches
Anecdotes and stories: from experience, as told by others
Thumbnail sketches:
    of famous people
    of places
    of content ideas
    of historical events
Guess who/what descriptions
Letters: personal reactions, observations, informational persuasive:
    to the editor
    to public officials
    to imaginary people
    from imaginary places
Requests
Applications

Memos
Resumés and summaries
Poems
Plays
Stories
Fantasy
Adventure
Science fiction
Historical stories
Dialogues and conversations
Children's books
Telegrams
Editorials
Commentaries
Responses and rebuttals
Newspaper "fillers"
Fact books or fact sheets
School newspaper stories
Stories or essays for local newspapers

*From Stephen Tchudi and Joanne Yates, *Teaching Writing in the Content Areas: Senior High School* (Washington, D.C.: National Education Association, 1983), p. 12. Used by permission.

Proposals
Case studies:
  school problems
  local issues
  national concerns
  historical problems
  scientific issues
Songs and ballads
Sculpture
Reviews:
  books (including texts)
  films
  outside reading
  television programs
  documentaries
Historical "you are there" scenes
Science notes:
  observations
  science notebooks
  reading reports
  lab reports
Math:
  story problems
  solutions to problems
  record books
  notes and observations
Responses to literature
Utopian proposals
Practical proposals
Interviews:
  actual
  imaginary

Directions:
  how-to
  school or neighborhood guide
  survival manual
Dictionaries and lexicons
Technical reports
Future options, notes on:
  careers, employment
  school and training
  military/public service
Written debates
Taking a stand:
  school issues
  family problems
  state or national issues
  moral questions
Books and booklets
Informational monographs
Radio scripts
TV scenarios and scripts
Dramatic scripts
Notes for improvised drama
Cartoons and cartoon strips
Slide show scripts
Puzzles and word searches
Prophecy and predictions
Photos and captions
Collage, montage
Mobiles

Tchudi's list is not exhaustive. A creative teacher can find many more ways of integrating writing activities into instruction in science, mathematics, health, or music. In the pages that follow, you will find some specific suggestions for most content areas. They are intended to demonstrate only a few ways in which writing to learn might work in your classroom.

The Language Arts

Teachers of English and foreign languages have responsibility for both writing to learn and learning to write. Balancing these roles can be a difficult task. There are three typical approaches to juggling these roles. The first, and least desirable, is to ignore one role or the other. The second is to integrate the roles by evaluating for technical correctness and content at the same time. This approach requires a highly structured system to be effective and is likely to present difficulties when trying to assign a grade. The third approach separates writing assignments into two types: those aimed at learning to write and those aimed at writing to learn. Thus, a paragraph written for the purpose of demonstrating proper form and technical correctness would be evaluated in one way; an entry in a personal journal would be handled in another.

Teachers of foreign languages are likely to have a greater need to emphasize learning to write at the secondary level than do teachers of English. Although there are exceptions, most students enter secondary school with the basic skills necessary to communicate in their native language. On the other hand, students of a foreign language generally spend their time on the basics of vocabulary and grammar. So until the students gain mastery of the basics of a language, it is unlikely that they will be able to write about content. However, once students show a sufficient mastery of a language, the teacher should put more emphasis on writing to learn. There may also be occasions in foreign language classes when writing in English can enhance student understanding of the application of a grammatical rule or a nuance of a particular culture. In such a case, writing to learn can be valuable tool.

Although the following activities could be utilized in a variety of ways depending on the specific content involved, they are equally applicable to both English and foreign language classes.

Journals

The practice of requiring students to keep personal journals is not new to teachers of English; indeed, it is an accepted approach. Students usually are free to write whatever they wish in a journal, but writing to learn is best served when student writing is directed toward a specific topic. In teaching a poetry unit, for example, a teacher might ask students to react privately in their journals to some idea expressed in a poem. This could be done in class or as a homework assignment. Writing to learn should help students to organize their own thoughts and to gain new insights. Students may wish to share their journal entries with the class or the teacher, and to write again on the same topic after a subsequent discussion.

Summaries

Students' understanding of the plot of a novel or short story may be enhanced by selecting a chapter or smaller portion of text and asking students to summarize in writing what has occurred. In novels that utilize a number of subplots, this technique can help students to follow the story. It also motivates students to read with attention to plot, and it can help the teacher to find out who is lost and who is not. Summaries require students to sort important events from trivial elements and to organize them in view of previous knowledge. After students have written their summaries, a discussion of the topic should prove fruitful. Writing to learn seems to prepare students better for class discussion. A creative variation of this activity is to ask students to write a feasible alternative plot sequence, having a character act in some other manner, and to prove in a class discussion that the alternative is viable.

Interviews

Writing an interview with a fictional character forces a student to delve into what makes a character "tick." Students in a Spanish class might be asked to write Don Quixote's response when asked to comment on what "Honor" means. One wonders what Lady Macbeth might reply to the same question. This activity requires the student writers to put themselves in the place of the character, to consider all that is known about the character, and to develop a logical response. By writing in the first person, the student empathizes with the character and may gain insight into areas of characterization previously overlooked. Whether writing a complete interview or the answer to a single question, the exercise forces students to think, synthesize, infer, and create through written expression.

The Social Sciences

The written word is as important to the social sciences as to the other content areas. Students in the social sciences need to be aware that when studying history, political science, or current events, words are powerful tools. Students need to be aware that documents like the U.S. Constitution are not thrown together haphazardly; they need to be aware that in matters of national diplomacy words are chosen with extreme care. Thus, in the social sciences it is important to emphasize precise writing.

The social sciences are well suited for a variety of writing activities. Research papers and essay responses to test questions can be effective learning tools. The social sciences are such a broad area that dozens of writing activities can be adapted to strengthen learning. So long as the activities are evaluated for clarity and completeness of content, rather than for grammatical correctness and proper spelling, there should be a positive impact on learning.

Letters to the Editor

Students of American history can assume the role of a historical character and write a letter to the editor concerning a historic event. A student in the role of an American patriot might prepare a scathing letter justifying the Boston Tea Party. Students might write from the viewpoint of a Virginia slave owner, justifying the institution of slavery. Letters need not be just to editors of newspapers. Students can take the role of one person writing to another; for example, a mother of a Union soldier killed at Gettysburg might write to President Lincoln to ask why her son had to die. Or a student might take Lincoln's role and answer such a plea. When preparing such letters, students must organize their facts and understand the events that they are writing about. It is impossible to describe something effectively when writing to someone else unless you understand it. In order to write effectively about the Boston Tea Party, the student would have to understand its causes. Transferring thoughts to paper through the writing process would help the student to understand the subject and assist the student in retaining the information.

Oral History

Since the publication of the first *Foxfire Book* by Eliot Wigginton in the early Seventies, oral history projects have become popular social science activities. Students have gone into their communities, rural and urban, to interview older citizens and to record various types of folklore. These interviews based on notes are also writing to learn. Students involved in recording a folktale from an old man back in the hills (even if a cassette recorder is used) must take great care to transcribe the tale correctly. Later, students may be called on to tailor it for publication in a *Foxfire*-type student publication. In preparing the tale for publication, they are likely to learn something about the art of storytelling. Students who are recording a process, like chair caning or dulcimer making, will learn to choose words carefully, to organize steps in the process, to define terms clearly, and to double-check for completeness. In such cases, clarity and completeness are essential; by putting the process into words, the students will understand it better themselves. It is worth noting that when publications by students are involved, the teacher or students assume an editorial role in which the mechanics of language become an important concern. In these situations, there is legitimate overlap between learning to write and writing to learn. Such a project is an excellent opportunity for cooperation between the social studies teacher and the English teacher.

Journals

Journals are an excellent means of bringing relevance to social science classes. Whether the subject is history, sociology, psychology, political science, or geography, students can benefit from writing

17

regularly in a personal journal on some topic related to the subject. Students in psychology might be asked to relate something from their personal experience to something being studied in class; students in American history might be asked to relate some historical event to what is happening in the world today. These activities will force students to think carefully about what they are learning in class and relate it to their daily lives. As they write their responses, which may be only a paragraph or two in a notebook, their understanding of behavior or of historical events will improve. Students might be asked to write on a topic of their choice or on teacher-directed topics and turn the journal in every two weeks or so for reading by the teacher. The teacher would read the entries and write a positive comment or two to encourage further writing, and thinking, by the student. The teacher would not grade the work or mark grammatical errors unless clarity was seriously affected. The journal is a highly flexible device that can be tailored to the teacher's instructional objectives. It can be another valuable tool for writing to learn.

The Sciences

The sciences readily lend themselves to the writing to learn approach. The ability to record completely and clearly the results of one's work is a skill that is as essential to students in the chemistry laboratory as it was to Edison or the Curies in their pioneering work. When writing up experiments, students need to be able to state clearly the purpose of their investigation and to define accurately the problem they are trying to solve. They must be able to outline their procedures, analyze their data, and put their conclusions into writing. Writing lab reports in chemistry, physics, biology, and general science classes requires students to follow a specified format and to use the specialized vocabulary of science.

Writing to learn in the sciences should go beyond the basic lab report. There are other, less formal types of writing that can also be used to enhance learning in the sciences. Consider the following.

Intermittent Paragraph Writing

Because scientific principles tend to build one on another, it is essential that students have a good understanding of one principle before proceeding further. One useful method for ensuring understanding is to provide a few minutes for students to write a paragraph or two following a short lecture on a scientific principle. For example, a lecture in biology dealing with the concept of osmosis might be followed with a five- to ten-minute period during which the students are asked to write a paragraph defining the term and how the process works. The students might also be asked to include an illustration or example. In responding to the assignment, the students will pull together the information from the lecture and integrate it with any prior knowledge they may have gained from past experiences or the textbook. By explaining the process in their own words, the students arrive at a clearer understanding of the process of osmosis.

If students are told at the start of the lecture that they will be writing afterward, they are likely to pay more attention, take more detailed notes, and generally perform better when tested on the material. The value of the activity lies in the thinking-learning-writing process that the student goes through to complete the assignment. The writing need not be graded; the teacher may not even wish to collect it. However, if the teacher chooses to collect the written work, it can provide insight into how well individual students understand the concept or principle. A quick evaluation of the written work will determine whether re-teaching is necessary.

Writing on Controversial Issues

Scientists are sometimes accused of being so interested in pursuing their research that they often do not concern themselves with the ethical/moral implications of their discoveries. It has been said that as the scientific and technical fields have become more specialized, the ethical side of science has been neglected. In science classes, studying such topics as nuclear energy or genetic engineering provides an opportunity for students to consider the ethical issues surrounding these controversial topics. Some teachers have done this through writing assignments that ask students to research thoroughly all sides of an issue, to present both sides clearly and completely in writing, and then to conclude with a statement of one's own position.

A class discussion alone does not allow everyone to say all that they would like to say regarding a controversial topic, but a writing assignment provides an opportunity for students to gather the facts and to synthesize their own positions on the issue. Such writing assignments encourage students to consider the ethical implications of scientific research, to develop skills of unbiased analysis and synthesis of data, and to see the relationships between what occurs in the laboratory and what happens in their daily lives. A term paper in a biology class dealing with the implications of genetic engineering could be a highly relevant learning experience for a student.

Limericks

Poetry is not the realm of only English teachers; a simple poetic form like the limerick also can be a learning experience in the science classroom. A teacher of general science might ask students to write a limerick that contains one scientific fact about a chemical element. An enterprising student might come up with something like this:

S is such a nice shade of yellow,
It looks somewhat like powdered jello.
Who ever would think
That when burned it would stink
And prove such a smelly old fellow.

Such an exercise can improve students' vocabulary, as well as help them to become familiar with the periodic table of elements. By highlighting a fact about each element and putting it in limerick form, students create a mnemonic device for learning the periodic table. If the limericks are posted on the bulletin board, other students can also memorize them.

Mathematics

It is a common misconception that writing skills and mathematics have little in common beyond the transcription of word problems. But much of the logic and organizational effort that goes into good writing parallels roughly the processes involved in solving math problems. Sometimes the best way to master a mathematical concept is to put it into one's own words; sometimes the best way to solve a math problem is to paraphrase it to clarify relationships. Computer programming, which is often part of the mathematics curriculum at the secondary level, accentuates the importance of clear and precise language because the computer has no leeway in interpreting commands. Computer language and precisely written English have a good deal in common, and the care required for even simple programming can rub off onto other forms of communication.

Simple Programming

When writing a simple computer program, the student not only learns the programming steps but also learns a good deal about the operation of language in general. In seeking to "de-bug" a program, students are doing a form of proofreading; they must revise the program much as the writer prepares a second draft. The goal of programmer and writer is the same: precise, clear language for the transmission of ideas. Such skills tend to transfer easily to other forms of communication because the student becomes more aware of the importance of clarity in communication. There is also benefit in having the student copy a short program longhand from the monitor, reflecting on each command and its effect as it is written.

Logic Problems

One effective way of promoting logical thinking is through the use of problems such as the following:

The crew of a certain train consists of a brakeman, a conductor, an engineer, and a fireman, whose names are Art, John, Pete, and Tom in no particular order.

- John is older than Art.
- The brakeman has no relatives on the crew.
- The engineer and the fireman are brothers.
- John is Pete's nephew.
- The fireman is not the conductor's uncle, and the conductor is not the engineer's uncle.

What position does each man hold, and how are the men related?*

In every classroom, there are always one or two students for whom such puzzles are easy; and there are a few who never solve them. In clarifying the logical process involved in the solution, ask the students who have solved it to write down the steps involved. Writing will clarify the process in their minds and provide a basis for leading slower students through the process; once the slower students understand the process, they should also be asked to write out the steps in detail. The activity will clarify the process, highlight any logical gaps, and increase the likelihood of retention of the logical concepts involved in solving similar problems.

Definitions

Mathematics has its own terminology. Students can benefit by writing paraphrases of the definitions of such terms as "axiom" and "theorem." When lecturing on congruency, the teacher may ask students to write their own definition of the term and give an example. Such an activity will help students to visualize geometric terms like "congruent" and will tend to clarify the meanings of more abstract concepts. When doing this simple activity, students will be forced to relate information from the lecture to what they already know and to organize and synthesize it so that the concept becomes their own.

---

*The correct solution is: Art is the brakeman, Pete is the engineer, Tom is the fireman, and John is the conductor. John is Tom's son and Pete's nephew; Art has no relatives on the crew.

The Industrial Arts

There are many areas in the industrial arts where writing to learn can enhance learning. Manipulative skills are probably best learned through "hands-on" demonstration and individual practice, but many skills may be learned better through reinforcement by selected writing activities.

Written Description of Processes

Writing can be an effective method for clarifying processes and procedures related to various aspects of industrial arts. Safety and maintenance procedures for the wood shop are more likely to be clear in the minds of students and more likely to be put into practice if students are asked to write them out in detail. Such writing forces students to identify each step of a process or procedure, to visualize it, and to develop it logically before moving on to describe the next step. Asking students to write can also ensure a clear and complete understanding of many facets of the manufacturing process, whether the product be a fine set of water skis or a tick-tack-toe board.

Written Interviews

Interviews of persons involved in various occupations can provide valuable career learning experiences for industrial arts students. Students need some preparation for conducting interviews. For example, a student who interviews a long-distance trucker should receive some guidance on the types of questions to ask, how to take notes, and how to convert those notes into a clear and complete report of the interview. The writing process will reinforce the information in the student's memory. And if the students are given a publications outlet for their interviews in the school paper or a career guidance bulletin, they will tend to give more careful thought to their writing.

R & D Reports

Many industrial arts teachers require their students to write "R & D" (Research and Development) reports on a wide variety of topics. A student might investigate anything from the relative merits of certain types of bridge construction to the comparative holding power of synthetic versus natural adhesives. Such an assignment requires the student to learn in detail about some facet of the industrial arts, and the writing of a report tends to increase both understanding and retention. In order to make a case for one type of bridge over another or for one adhesive over another, students must clearly understand the data they have gathered. Writing requires organization and synthesis of data in order to produce a clear and complete report. Once again, learning is enhanced through the writing process itself.

Business and Vocational Studies

Communicating effectively with others is a key factor for success in business, as it is in other careers. Much of the communication carried on by businesses, regardless of size, is in the form of writing. The president of a company must be able to put ideas into writing clearly and effectively; the chief production engineer must be able to write clear and complete work orders for the production crew. Effective management requires skillful communication, both face-to-face and in writing.

Teachers of business and vocational subjects need to help students master basic communication skills. Every student needs to know how to prepare a resumé, complete a job application, and write a basic business letter. Such organizations as the American Industrial Arts Association and the Vocational and Industrial Clubs of America have long recognized the importance of communication skills for their student members. They sponsor national, state, district, and local speech contests to provide opportunities for students to develop both verbal and written skills. The student who prepares to speak in a contest is involved in a writing-thinking process that promotes learning. Even those persons in the technical vocations, such as auto mechanics, require good reading skills for interpreting directions in manuals, good speaking skills for dealing with customers, and good writing skills for preparing a work order. As citizens and consumers, students need writing skills to communicate outside the workplace as well as on the job.

Case Studies

Case studies can serve as valuable learning tools in many business and vocational areas. A student who is asked to write about a particular case is likely to learn more and give more thought to a solution. Whether the case deals with the diagnosis of a problem in an automobile engine or a complaint from a nursing home patient, the student can benefit from writing about it. Such writing may then serve as a basis for a class discussion of the case.

Process Descriptions

Changing spark plugs, centering a letter on a typewriter, and performing CPR are all processes, the learning of which can be enhanced if students are required to detail in writing the steps involved. The writing process will increase retention by forcing students to visualize the steps in chronological order as they write. Gaps in learning can be spotted easily if students are asked to exchange papers and check each other's paper for accuracy. Such peer evaluation tends to promote both clarity and completeness in student writing.

Business Letters

The writing of simple business letters is a skill that everyone needs at one time or another. When students take a secretarial role and are asked to prepare a business letter for their employer, they are going through the same process as students writing essay responses to an exam question. They are sorting, organizing, and synthesizing data in order to prepare a complete and clearly written communication. They have to consider their audience and the effect they want to have on that audience. Writing business letters is both a learning to write (in a business style) and a writing to learn exercise. Writing and replying to other students' letters can be a worthwhile activity in vocational and business classes.

Health and Physical Education

The health curriculum, with its concern for systems of the body, principles for practicing good health, and processes like CPR, is well suited to the writing to learn approach. Writing to learn also can contribute substantially to the physical education program. A good physical education program involves more than just having the students engage in team sports; it will also acquaint students with a variety of sports activities that can be pursued throughout their lives. Writing to learn is especially useful as a method for encouraging students to investigate different sports that they can pursue after they graduate. In these areas, as in others, the use of writing activities can enhance learning and contribute to improvement of overall writing skills.

Fictitious Interviews

Although there are many opportunities in the health curriculum for real interviews, students may enjoy writing a fictitious interview with one of the body's organs. When studying the effects of drugs or alcohol on the brain, a student might interview a group of brain cells who relate what happened to them and some of their "gray matter" friends as a result of a drink or two. In order to create dialogue for the interview, the student would have to read and understand material dealing with the effects of alcohol on the brain. Writing the dialogue would ensure clear understanding as well as retention of the material. Similar interviews could be conducted with the stomach, the lungs, or other parts of the body.

Reactions to Film/Video Materials

There are many fine 16mm and videotape resources available in the area of health. Some using remarkable microphotography techniques allow students to see into the body itself and to examine the workings of the heart, the circulatory system, and other body systems in detail. Other films that deal with smoking, drug abuse, automotive safety, and other topics offer judgmental messages, some of which turn students off. One way of ensuring complete class participation, as well as serious thought about a given topic, is to require students to react in writing to what they have seen. You might consider having students keep a "Reaction Log" in which they would write a paragraph or two about the film. Such writing could be done in or outside the classroom. The teacher should collect the logs periodically and, using positive written comments, react to what students have written. Such a log can be a valuable and relevant learning experience for the student, as well as for the teacher.

Procedural Descriptions

Perhaps the most valuable lessons a student can learn in a health class relate to life-saving procedures such as the Heimlich Maneuver and cardio-pulmonary resuscitation (CPR). Students need to see such techniques demonstrated and have an opportunity to practice them. Like actors preparing for opening night, they need to "overlearn" the procedures until they become second nature. One way to enhance retention of these procedures and to ensure complete learning is to ask students to write out the procedure in detail, describing what happens at each step. Students who receive adequate practice and enhance that practice by writing to learn will be more likely to know automatically what to do when the moment arrives.

The teacher of physical education should be concerned with building positive attitudes toward exercise and physical activity that students will continue to enjoy as they grow older. A steady diet of basketball, volleyball, and baseball may provide activity for them now, but after graduation their opportunities for team sports will be more limited. Students need to develop a love for activities that will keep them physically fit in their twenties, thirties, forties, and beyond. One way of providing exposure to such activities is to plan teaching units that offer students a "smorgasbord" of activities in which each student has a chance to sample each activity for a day or two. If resources do not permit exposure to a wide variety of activities, the next best solution is to assign outside reading or viewing of such activities and require students to write about them. There are numerous print resources that cover everything from how to play a sport and how to improve your skills to sports fiction and biographies. With the excellent coverage of all types of individual and team events on television, even rural students can see the finest ice skaters, gymnasts, and runners. Students can be asked to read about or view certain sports activities and react in writing. They can discuss what they found attractive about a sport, what they did not enjoy, and whether they would like to give it a try. Such writing assignments will force students to think seriously about making physical activities a continuing part of their lives.

Art and Music

While the teaching of art and music in secondary schools is very performance oriented, there are areas where writing activities can contribute to learning. In art history and music history, there are dozens of possible writing activities, from writing biographies to creating limericks using music or art terms. There are also opportunities for interdisciplinary efforts in art and music history, where students can study and write about the influence of such movements as Impressionism and Expressionism, which strongly affected both fields. Creative teachers of art and music will use a variety of writing activities to awaken young minds to other areas of interest in these two fields.

Biographies

The lives of such artists as Michelangelo, Manet, and Gauguin provide fascinating subject matter for a variety of writing activities. Likewise, the lives of Mozart, Beethoven, and Tchaikovsky offer fertile ground for study as well. Students can write on such questions as why a given artist or musician painted or composed as he did, or how Beethoven, who was deaf, was able to compose such great works. A student might discuss the ways in which a certain artist or musician was representative of his age. In any case, students who answer questions raised while reading a biography will not only learn something about the people portrayed, but also will ponder some of the larger questions related to any act of artistic creation.

Written Reactions to Works

Works as diverse as Tchaikovsky's *The Nutcracker Suite* and Henry Mancini's *March of the Cue Balls* are likely to stir up varied images in the minds of young listeners, as will the paintings of Picasso or Dali. If students have no previous familiarity with such works, they will likely show a great degree of creativity and imagination if asked to write their personal reactions in a journal or as a special assignment. With practice, students can learn to develop effective moods through word choice and sentence structure that accurately reflect their reactions.

Writing About Outside Interests

With proper guidance students can be assigned to write a paper on some phase of music or art that is not covered in depth in the curriculum. Students may wish to explain the differences between Renaissance and Classical musical styles, or they may want to investigate country music, jazz, folk music, or instruments. A budding artist may wish to learn more about sculpture, working in metals, or another field of art. Music and art are such broad areas that they offer something for everyone; students only need someone to start them on the right road. The resources for outside reading are there, but reading alone is not sufficient. Students who are asked to write about what they have read will put more thought into the project, and they are more likely to find personal relevance in what is learned. Students also are more likely to retain what is learned through writing. The concerned teacher will ask students of music and the arts to read and write about topics related to those fields. In our performance-oriented secondary school programs, this is the only way in which nonperforming students with interest in the arts are likely to discover the breadth and depth of these fields.

Home Economics

Once characterized by cooking, sewing, and personal care, home economics today covers myriad topics, from design and fashion merchandising to consumerism and family relationships. Today's broad home economics curriculum has many opportunities for the use of writing in the classroom.

Television Script Writing

Students might develop their own "Galloping Gourmet" 30-minute television program for a unit on foods and cooking. In developing the script and commercials for such a program, students would learn a great deal about food and videotape production. Students would need to understand thoroughly the recipe and the process involved to develop a clear and complete written script, and they would be forced to consider what is happening as the process is followed. Camera directions are needed, and the dialogue must be coordinated with the action. If commercials are also included, there will be opportunity for creative humor. To develop a 30-minute program, students would have to pay attention to timing and make a careful selection of words and content. Such an experience would be enjoyable for students; and it would complement units of study that deal with television, advertising, and cooking.

A Day in the Life of. . .

As students investigate the career possibilities in home economics, a good activity is to ask them to research thoroughly a career field of their choice and then to write a narrative describing a fictional workday for themselves in that role. In order for such a narrative to be accurate, the writer will need a thorough understanding of the career field and its everyday expectations. Someone writing about being a dietitian in a nursing home will need to investigate thoroughly that role in order to write effectively about it; the interested student might wish to interview a dietitian to gain first-hand insight into the job. Such a writing assignment requires a high degree of organizational skill, knowledge of the terminology used in that career area, and clear descriptive prose. In completing such an assignment, the student will gain a great deal more insight than could come from simply reading about the career. Writing about the career field in concrete terms makes the assignment personally relevant.

Written Reactions to Films

There are many excellent films available on aging and family relationships for use in home economics classrooms. One example is *Peege* (1974), which is about a family's Christmas visit to their stroke-crippled grandmother, nicknamed "Peege," who lives in a nursing home. It is a moving film about love and the roles grandmothers play in our lives, as seen through the eyes of the family members. It frequently brings tears to the eyes of students and forces students to think seriously about their own family relationships. This kind of film makes students want to react in writing at a personal level and to re-examine their relationships with parents and grandparents. While the writing serves as an excellent prelude to class discussion, it is a highly relevant personal learning experience in itself. Such a writing exercise is well suited to a personal journal that is read by the teacher only at the invitation of the student. Such private writing encourages personal growth.

A Final Note

Writing to learn is just beginning to be used extensively at the secondary level, but we now know that writing activities are powerful tools for classroom learning. Still, there is a great deal that we do not know about that mysterious thinking-learning-transcribing process we call writing. If you have a strong interest to learn more about writing to learn, you might consult some of the sources listed in the bibliography. They are good places to start. Once you understand what writing to learn is all about, then you can examine your own curriculum and incorporate appropriate writing activities. Remember that the emphasis is on the applications of writing as a learning tool; improvements in writing skills will occur coincidentally, but they do occur.

Bibliography

Britton, James, et al. *The Development of Writing Abilities (11-18)*. Urbana, Ill.: National Council of Teachers of English, 1975.

Delmar, P. Jay. "Composition and the High School: Steps Toward Facultywide Involvement." *English Journal* 67 (November 1978): 36-38.

Emig, Janet. *The Composing Processes of Twelfth Graders*. Urbana, Ill.: National Council of Teachers of English, 1971.

Emig, Janet. "Writing As a Mode of Learning." *College Composition and Communication* 122 (1977).

Fulwiler, Toby, and Young, Art, eds. *Language Connections: Writing and Reading Across the Curriculum*. Urbana, Ill.: National Council of Teachers of English, 1983.

Goswami, Dixie, and Butler, Maureen, eds. *The Web of Meaning: Essays on Writing, Teaching, Learning, and Thinking*. Montclair, N.J.: Boynton/Cook, 1983.

Graser, Elsa R. *Teaching Writing: A Process Approach*. Dubuque, Iowa: Kendall/Hunt, 1983.

Hennings, Dorothy Grant. *Teaching Communication and Reading Skills in the Content Areas*. Bloomington, Ind.: Phi Delta Kappa, 1982.

Howie, Sherry H. *A Guidebook for Teaching Writing in the Content Areas*. Rockleigh, N.J.: Allyn and Bacon, 1983.

Kean, John M. *The Teaching of Writing in Our Schools* (fastback #193). Bloomington, Ind.: Phi Delta Kappa Educational Foundation, 1983.

Knoblauch, C.H., and Brannon, Lil. "Writing as Learning Through the Curriculum." *College English* 45 (September 1983): 465-474.

Maimon, Elaine, et al. *Writing in the Arts and Sciences*. Cambridge, Mass.: Winthrop, 1981.

Odell, L. "The Process of Writing and the Process of Learning." *College Composition and Communication* 42 (1980).

Tchudi, Stephen, and Huerta, Margie. *Teaching Writing in the Content Areas: Middle School/Junior High*. Washington, D.C.: National Education Association, 1983.

Tchudi, Stephen, and Yates, Joanne. *Teaching Writing in the Content Areas: Senior High School*. Washington, D.C.: National Education Association, 1983.

This fastback and others in the series are made available at low cost through the Phi Delta Kappa Educational Foundation, established in 1966 with a bequest from George H. Reavis. The foundation exists to promote a better understanding of the nature of the educative process and the relation of education to human welfare.

Single copies of fastbacks are 75¢ (60¢ to Phi Delta Kappa members). Write to Phi Delta Kappa, Eighth and Union, Box 789, Bloomington, IN 47402 **for quantity discounts for any title or combination of titles.**

PDK Fastback Series Titles

(Continued on inside back cover)

See inside back cover for prices.